I'm A Jew, Are You?

I'M A JEW, ARE YOU?

Ain't Got No Press

Layout and Design ~ Rick Lupert
Cover Photo ~ Nicole Harvey
Back Cover Photo ~ Mike Daily

(818) 904-1021

or

15522 Stagg Street
Van Nuys, CA 91406

or

Rick@PoetrySuperHighway.com

Special thanks to Amélie Frank and Cassowary Press
for originally publishing this book

"The Poet" originally appeared in *I Am My Own Orange County* (Ain't Got No Press), "Apartment" originally appeared in *Beyond The Valley of the Contemporary Poets 1996 Anthology* (Sacred Beverage Press), "Goodbye Couch" originally appeared in *Brendan Constantine & Rick Lupert Tour parts of The World Official Souvenir Program* (Ain't Got No Press.), "Jesus, I'm Coming Home" originally appeared in the first issue of (sic) vice & verse Magazine.

Fifth CreateSpace Edition ~ June 2008
ISBN: 978-0-9727555-1-1 $8.00

Visit Lupert: It's The Website and The Poetry Super Highway
http://PoetrySuperHighway.com/

Contents

*The important part
of the journey is not
the destination.*

The Poet

The poet
got up to read
took off all his clothes
read naked

I could tell right away
he wasn't Jewish

Jesus, We're Coming Home

I
Group of Jews in Christian camp
Rented for weekend
      mountains
      snow
In stone amphitheater
crucifix embossed on
cold stage ground
      Jesus,
      are you buried
      here too?
Remember Jerusalem
Church of Holy Sepulcher
True burial place?
Jesus has network of
underground tunnels
Can rise anywhere he wants
      Not that we believe
      that sort of thing.

II
The Christian caretakers
are so hospitable they'd
convert if we asked them

III
Christian Steve shovels
dirt and snow
cleaning the way as if
we're the second coming

IV
Christian Steve communicates with
others via walkie talkie
    "Steve,
    come in.
    This is Jesus,
    Your Savior,
    breaker breaker."
    "Yes Lord,
    This is Steve"
    "We need more Mr. Pibb
    in the dining hall" says Jesus
    "I'm on my way
    oh Heavenly Master."

V
Steve has passed the shoveling off
to a Jewish volunteer.
The Jew sings
    "Workin' all night
    master's got me shovelin'
    ARGH"
We are Jews
in a Christian camp
singing Negro spirituals
like Pirates.
One world, one people.

VI
At the Christian camp
there is an unlimited refill soda bar.
Clearly, they are
not Buddhists.

VII
We post Israeli flags along
the Christian camp entry road.
It doesn't matter.
Come Sunday we'll have to
withdraw from this land too.

Apartment

I have two roommates
one is a Christian
one is a Muslim
and I am a Jew.
Our apartment is the old city,
Jerusalem.

Hanging in the Christian's room is a crucifix,
In the Muslim's room is a poster of people
        praying in Mecca,
and in my room, there is an Israeli flag,
and sometimes a giant gefilte fish.

Sometimes the Christian comes into my room
and accuses me of killing his messiah,
only in this case, it's Ella Fitzgerald.
Although everyone knows that Ella Fitzgerald
        died of old age,
her death remains a source of awkwardness
        between us.

Once I threatened to annex the Muslim's bedroom
unless he withdrew
the garbage from the kitchen.
He responded by blowing up my bathroom.
No-one was injured except for my cat
whose whiskers where a little singed.
I declared an apartment-wide day of remembrance
for my cat's heroic deeds.
Why not?

I have so many holidays,
What's one more?

Amidst all the turbulence,
we still manage to pay rent and share resources,
Water . . . food . . . cable.
We're catching up with the west
and our apartment exists as a paradigm for world
peace.

Goodbye Couch

You come to my house and
take my couch. I become
melancholy thinking of
couch history.

All the sittings upon
of the couch, the lyings upon
of the couch, the tv watchings
from the couch

It is a good couch
It form fitted to my bottom
Put me through college with
the change found beneath its cushions.
Never complained about anything
ever

Now it too looks melancholy
It's cloth perhaps a touch droopy
as it's carried out to your truck
on its way to your home.

It seems to cry to me
"Why me?
Why not take the other couch?
Have I not been a good couch?
Have my years of bounce retention
gone unnoticed?
Why not take the other couch?
Is it because I'm a Jew?"

I answer
"No couch,
you have been a good couch
You have cushioned my tushy
above and beyond,
provided endless snoozes
You are the couchiest of couches.

But couches, like lives
experience transition
to new lives
new living rooms
new asses.
You will go to the house of a
younger man where
your couchly prowess will be fully realized.
You will seat princes
and possibly women.
You will evolve to
Supreme being of the furniture kingdom.
It will be difficult at first
But as with all things you will
end up stronger, wiser.

Go couch
Go now
Go in the truck
Go to your new triumphant landscape
Goodbye couch
I will miss you.

The Eating of the Jews

It is the new year
and I am driving home
from Rosh Ha Shanah morning services.
I will rest until the evening
when I will join friends for the festive meal.

We Jews eat like Italians.
We have special foods for every holiday.
Symbolic foods.
Foods that make a statement to God
as they travel into our mouths.

Have you ever really thought about matzah?
I have.
It's intense.
Matzah has so much meaning
it makes the dictionary seem like a Canadian.

We even have special foods to eat
when nothing special is happening.
Let's talk kugle, kishke, falafel.
Don't ask what kishke is,
but Kugle,
I could go on about kugle for days.

I will be well fed tonight.
There will be potato dishes
that would kill most Anglos,
and apples dipped in so much honey
the new year will be sweet enough
to last through the naming of all our children.

To be a Jew is to eat
like our ancestors before us ate.
Are you hungry?

Messiah

The Jews are a people waiting for the Messiah
Every Morning I wake up and ask

"Has he come yet?"

Once the answer came
"No, but he called
left this message:

'Stop waiting

You are your own Messianic age
Live every moment as if I was there
Then you'll realize
        I already am.
I'm coming to your house for lunch
I hear you make great French Toast
I take my coffee black
I am the Messiah
Let the good times roll.'"

Jessi

for Jessi

It is Shabbat and
a week ago, Shabbat with you
Arizona girl, just my size,
once asked a bus driver to stop
so she could get out and pick a sunflower.
True story. It's like God read my profile
and said "Here, this is for you."

We've got memories dating back for days.
Like remember that time on the couch Sunday night?
Yeah, that was nice.
Now it's a week.
Me a thousand miles away
sitting in empty room
next to unlit candles.

It is cold,
like it was in the couch room,
until we got there.
I could turn on the heater
but who wants to do that?

Oh, sunflower girl
they add letters to your name
that have no business being there
But I can spell it
and speak it.
It's the only word I know,
Jessi.

Chi Damage

In my letter to the Coca-cola Corporation
I explained that a Buddhist friend
told me that Coca-cola kills your Chi and asked
what they were planning on doing about it.
They responded with an envelope
          full of consumer information
and a letter claiming that there is room in any diet
for pleasant soft drinks.
There was no mention of Chi or Buddhism.
I was going to write them back
and ask them why they ignore the Buddhists
and their theory of the essence of life
But I never got around to it
because the damage to my Chi
was already too extensive.

Sasquatch Comes to Seder

I invited Sasquatch to Seder
He said "Don't you think I'll
weird people out what with
all the fur and the
big feet?"

I answered "Nah,
we're Reform."

Whoopi

The ghosts of
several famous dead people
came to my house last week and
demanded that I
make them sandwiches.

I won't mention who they were
I have nothing to prove.

Goldberg

We swap stories
of dead plants we've known
You put your arm around me
like you did yesterday
tell me I smell Good
tell you You feel Good
You know
exactly when to touch me

So You're My Cousin

So you're my cousin
I say to the thirty-nine year old man
across the table who I haven't seen
in twenty one years
Apparently he came from the
tall side of the family.

> I was seven the last time I saw him
> He was younger too.
> We both seem to come from
> the hairy side of the family

Our reunion:
We walk extensively through a mall
The girls shop in *every* shop
Everyone buys shoes
except me.
Suddenly,
my cousin buys me shoes
Now, everyone has new shoes.

> We take pictures
> Tell stories of our entire lives
> Eat lunch
> Almost stop for coffee
> but at the last minute
> have dinner instead.

So you're my cousin
I say over and over
I needed him to assure me
It had been so long
as if I'd come from a family
with no relatives.

Cousin Addendum

> My cousin works in construction
> Offers to put in hardwood floors for me
> Wherever I go.
>
> Blood is thicker than commission.

I Come From Eastern Europe

I've got so much body hair,
It's not even funny

I've got so much body hair,
a chimpanzee looked at me and fainted

I've got so much body hair,
in the dictionary next to the word deforestation,
there is NOT a picture of me,

I've got so much body hair,
I need to buy two airplane tickets
even when I'm not going anywhere.

I've got so much body hair,
Telly Savalas used to wear me on his head
to pick up chicks

I've got so much body hair,
the people at Norelco have labeled me
public enemy number one

I've got so much body hair,
I don't need to wear clothing,
in fact I never do
see what I mean?
That's a lot of body hair.

I've got so much body hair
It's not even funny

Hair Addendum

Unlike Sampson,
If I were to cut my hair
I would still have all my power
because my power comes from my ass.
This is why I will never have
an assectomy

Former Camper Encounter

A former camper
comes up to me at the café
He's about to start college
Says he just picked his classes
at Santa Barbara
He's taking History of Japan Through Art
I tell him that
all the world's history
should be studied through art.

Suddenly
there is an understanding between us
Makes up for all the times
I found him out of his cabin
after hours

Former Student Encounter

I see a former student at the café
he looks like a Polish immigrant
wearing an Escher t-shirt
He never used to look like that.

The kids today...

Little Girl Future

As I sang songs with children
a little girl raised her hand
and asked me

Why do you not play the violin?

as if it was the most important question
in the world

Do you play the violin?

I asked.

She answered

I will in two years.

Genesis

In the beginning of creation
God made the Heavens and The Earth
Then came the real estate agents
and that pretty much
fucked everything up.

Exile

A man I knew
came up to me
at the table
and told me
I always seem like
I'm in a great state of solitude

I told him that I
had exiled myself
from civilization
and have chosen
to live out my exile
amongst people
in crowded cafés
like this one.

Big Man, Little Bagel

Big Man eats little bagel
Bagel is really full sized bagel
But man is so big,
bagel is dwarfed in his hand
Bagel looks like Fisher Price Bagel
next to big man
Big man looks silly eating little bagel
Like Arnold Schwarzeneggar
at a five year old's underwater tea party
Like Mr. T
being dainty

Hindu Gods Are Always Happy

Ganesa,
always with a grand elephant grin
underneath his trunk

Siva,
with his many arms and faces
grinning from mouth, to mouth, to mouth
thinking "I can do anything with these"
flailing all his arms with abandon

Visnu,
with his satisfied smirk
over his big tummy
as if to say
"I've eaten well today."

and

Parvati,
smiling over her ample bosom,
knowing
all the other Gods want her.

Conversation With God

Rick   "What are you up to tomorrow?"

God   "Everything."

Rick   "Can we get together?"

God   "I can make time."

Rick   "I've heard that about you."

My Precious Tummy

When a four year old
gives you a hug
and she looks up into your eyes
her head resting on your tummy
and she says

"It's So Nice and Soft"

you start to feel ok
with your increasing
stomach line.

Debbie Friedman The Cat

I'm going to get a cat
I'm going to get a cat and
name it Debbie Friedman
My cat is going to be
Debbie Friedman the Cat

Debbie Friedman is a Jewish Singer
Everybody loves Debbie Friedman

Debbie Friedman has a dog
Not me.
I'm going to have
Debbie Friedman *the cat*

Debbie Friedman the cat will not be a singer
Debbie Friedman the cat will not be Jewish
Not until after the neutering

Debbie Friedman the Cat will
travel to Israel and hang out in the streets
with all the other Jerusalem cats.
Debbie Friedman the cat will have a
better understanding of her heritage
than the other cats.

She will construct a replica of
The Western Wall in her litter box
with source materials
she will provide herself

Debbie Friedman the cat will
terrorize all the goldfish in the house
All of the goldfish in the house will also
be named Debbie Friedman
There will be Debbie Friedman the Goldfish One
through Debbie Friedman the Goldfish Six.
They will be happy goldfish
Except when Debbie Friedman the cat terrorizes them.

Debbie Friedman the cat will be a fluffy cat

Debbie Friedman the cat will never buy
Michael Jackson recordings

Debbie Friedman the cat will define cat spirituality

Everyone will love
Debbie Friedman the cat.

Everything Is Jewish

In the place where I pray
Everything is Jewish
The lizards
have all been circumcised
You can tell because
one just ran by without a tail.
Lizard moils are not very skilled.

The Squirrels only gather
Kosher acorns
This is a given because
all acorns are automatically Kosher.
Squirrels don't have to
worry about being traif.

The trees make the third Temple
Far away from Jerusalem
they become the southWestern american Wall

That Eucalyptus tree is the Holy of Holies
Where the Lizard priests make
important Halachic decisions

In the place where I pray
Everything is Jewish
The sound of the wind against the leaves is
the chanting of the Torah

Every day in nature
I become more and more religious.

I Still Believe

Ani ma-amin
Six million dead
Ani ma-amin
One and a half million children
Ani ma-amin
Piles of shoes found without feet
Ani ma-amin
So many shoes
Ani ma-amin
The children of Terezin exterminated
Ani ma-amin
never knowing
their poems would be turned into songs
that we will sing forever

Ani ma-amin
Ani-ma-amin
Im Kol Zeh, Ani -ma-amin

Even amidst all this,
I still believe

אֲנִי מַאֲמִין
עִם כָּל זֶה אֲנִי מַאֲמִין

(Hebrew text: Maimonides, 12th Century)

Havdallah

for Danny Maseng

I dip a finger in Saturday night's wine
brush it across both eyelids
as tears succumb to the inevitability
of Sabbath gravity
down
down
wet cheeks
Separation
away
Everything I see is holy

Rick's Other Books

A Man With No Teeth Serves Us Breakfast
Ain't Got No Press
May, 2007

I'd Like to Bake Your Goods
Ain't Got No Press
January, 2006

STOLEN MUMMIES
Ain't Got No Press
February, 2003

BRENDAN CONSTANTINE IS MY KIND OF TOWN
Inevitable Press
September, 2001

up liberty's skirt
Cassowary Press
March, 2001

FEEDING HOLY CATS
Cassowary Press
May, 2000

MOWING FARGO
Sacred Beverage Press
December, 1998

Lizard King of the Laundromat
The Inevitable Press
February, 1998

A 9' El Gja GeTaZX ;bhagl
Ain't Got No Press
May, 1997

Paris: It's The Cheese
Ain't Got No Press
May, 1996

For more information: http://PoetrySuperHighway.com/

www.ingramcontent.com/pod-product-compliance
Lightning Source LLC
Chambersburg PA
CBHW051050030426
42339CB00006B/289